Exploration of California

Serena Haines

Consultants

Kristina Jovin, M.A.T.
Alvord Unified School District
Teacher of the Year

Bijan Kazerooni, M.A.
Department of History
Chapman University

Publishing Credits

Rachelle Cracchiolo, M.S.Ed., *Publisher*
Conni Medina, M.A.Ed., *Managing Editor*
Emily R. Smith, M.A.Ed., *Series Developer*
June Kikuchi, *Content Director*
Marc Pioch, M.A.Ed., and Susan Daddis, M.A.Ed., *Editors*
Courtney Roberson, *Senior Graphic Designer*

Image Credits: Cover and p.1 National Gallery of Art; pp.2–3 Library of Congress [g3200.ct000725C]; pp.5 (foreground), 9 North Wind Picture Archives; p.5 (background) Library of Congress [g4410.ct000196]; p.6 (bottom) Library of Congress [g3200.ct000725C]; pp.6–7, 20 (front), 29 (middle) Granger, NYC; p.8 (left) CarverMostardi/Alamy Stock Photo, (right) Wallace Collection, London, UK/Bridgeman Images; p.10 NASA Earth Observations Laboratory, Johnson Space Center; p.11 Stock Montage, Inc./Alamy Stock Photo; p.12 (front) Los Angeles Public Library Photo Collection; p.13 (top) Album/sfgp/Newscom; p.14 Photo by Chris Stone/Times of San Diego; p.15 Encyclopaedia Britannica/UIG Universal Images Group/Newscom; p.17 Stephen Saks Photography/Alamy Stock Photo; pp.18–19 Library of Congress [LC-DIG-highsm-21575]; p.19 (front) Public domain ca. 17th century; pp.20-21 Universal Images Group North America LLC/Alamy Stock Photo; p.22 Black Gold Cooperative Library System; p.23 Sarin Images/Granger, NYC; p.24 (top) Library of Congress [det.4a31561]; pp.24–25 Library of Congress [LC-DIG-ppmsca-17978]; pp.26, 29 (bottom) UCLA, Library Special Collections, Charles E. Young Research Library; p.28 World History Archive/Newscom; p.29 (top) Library of Congress [g4410.ct000196]; p.32 Album/sfgp/Newscom; all other images from iStock and/or Shutterstock.

Library of Congress Cataloging-in-Publication Data
Names: Haines, Serena, author.
Title: Exploration of California / Serena Haines.
Description: Huntington Beach, CA : Teacher Created Materials, [2018] | Includes index. | Audience: Grades 4-6.
Identifiers: LCCN 2017014090 (print) | LCCN 2017015235 (ebook) | ISBN 9781425835033 (eBook) | ISBN 9781425832339 (pbk.)
Subjects: LCSH: California--Discovery and exploration--Juvenile literature. | California--History--To 1846--Juvenile literature.
Classification: LCC F851.5 (ebook) | LCC F851.5 .H45 2018 (print) | DDC 979.4/04--dc23
LC record available at https://lccn.loc.gov/2017014090

Teacher Created Materials
5301 Oceanus Drive
Huntington Beach, CA 92649-1030
http://www.tcmpub.com

ISBN 978-1-4258-3233-9

Printed in China
Nordica.042019.CA21900332

Table of Contents

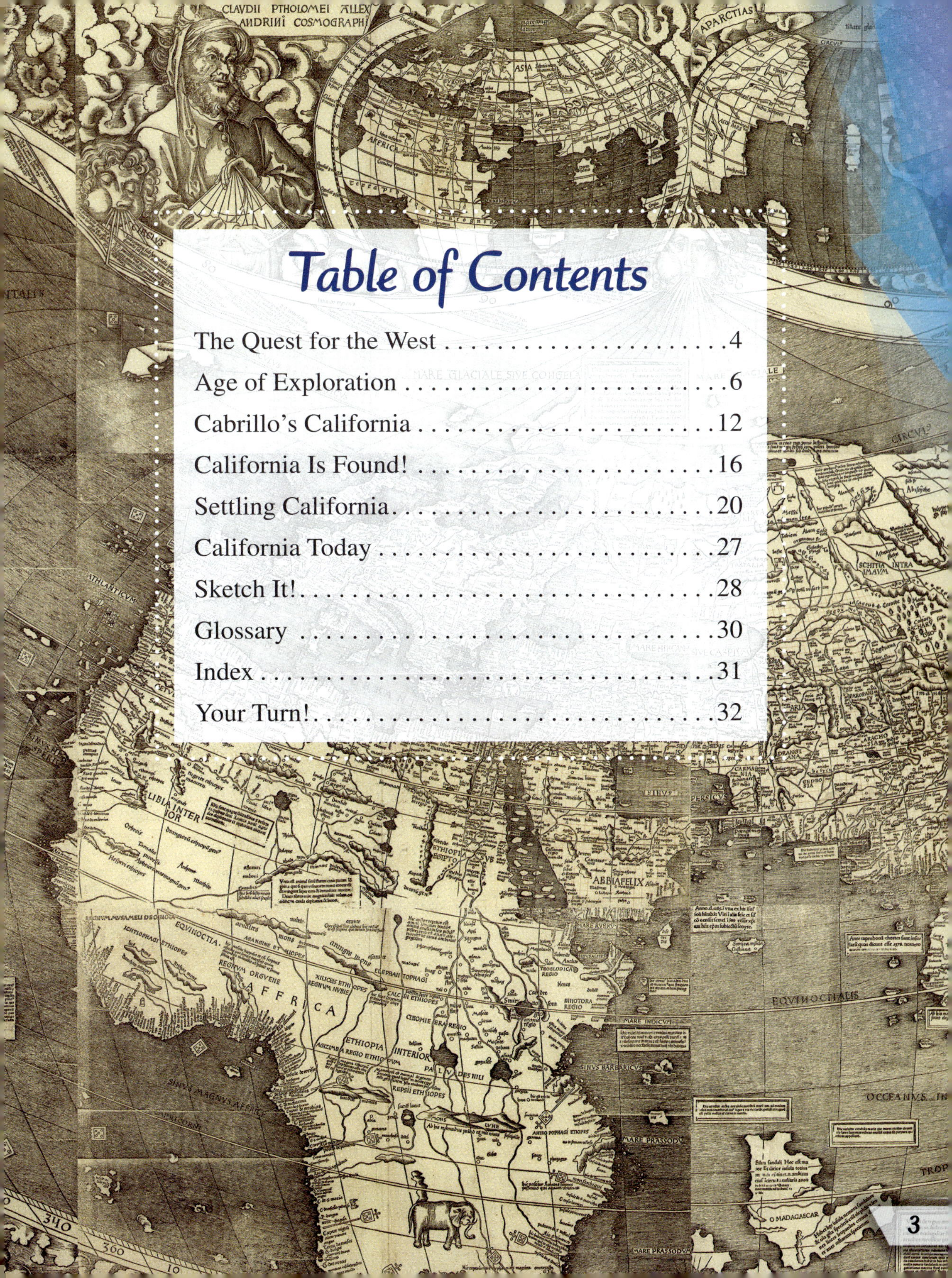

The Quest for the West

Imagine a place with mountains made of gold. Warrior women are the only ones who live there. The beautiful and powerful Queen Calafia rules them. Her kingdom is called *California*. This was a **myth** that some people in Europe heard about this faraway land. No one had ever been there. It sounded like a dream.

Stories like this made people want to explore the world. Explorers like Marco Polo inspired others. Polo was from Italy. He traveled to China, India, and other parts of Asia. He brought back silks and spices to the people of Europe. In 1298, he published a book about his adventures. His book encouraged people to search for new and faster routes to Asia. Some explorers tried heading west. These explorers did not find a new route to Asia. But they did find new lands.

Silks and Spices

Explorers were in search of spices and fabrics. Although it is hard to imagine now, spices like cinnamon, nutmeg, and pepper were very precious then. People were willing to pay small fortunes for them.

Economics

This 1720 map shows that some people believed California was an island!

Not an Island

No one from Europe had ever seen California. People used to think it was an island. That is what early maps showed. In 1747, King Ferdinand VI of Spain told his people that California is not an island. That is how a myth that had been around for over two centuries ended.

Geography

Marco Polo

Age of Exploration

The Age of Exploration began in the early 1400s. This time is also known as the *Age of Discovery*. This is because many Europeans discovered and explored parts of the world that were unknown to them. Explorers from Portugal, Spain, England, France, and the Netherlands all raced each other. They hoped to bring the riches of Asia back to their home countries. And, they all wanted to be the first to do so.

Henry the Navigator was a prince from Portugal. In 1415, he sailed around the coast of Africa. These waters were unsafe and choppy. He was the first to take this route. New maps, ships, and inventions, such as the compass, helped him find his way.

Portugal's biggest **rival** at the time was Spain. Both kings hoped to expand their **empires** around the world. In 1492, Spain's king supported his own explorer. His name was Christopher Columbus. He took a chance and sailed west. After 10 long, hard weeks at sea, he set foot in the New World. His voyage was a huge turning point in history.

Naming America

A map of the New World was made in 1507. The name "America" was chosen for the large **landmass** that would become North and South America. The name came from Italian explorer Amerigo Vespucci (ves-PYOO-chee). It was believed he was the first one to find the new land. They were wrong, but the name stuck!

Spanish Sailing Ships

Spanish explorers sailed on ships called *galleons*. Galleons were used for both trade and battle. With three main **masts**, they could speed through the water. Galleons had plenty of cargo space to bring back gold and other treasures found in the New World.

Soldiers of Fortune

The **conquistadors** (kon-KEES-tah-dors) were soldiers for Spain. They sailed to the New World in search of gold and land for their king. Conquistadors were very advanced for their time. They wore shirts made of **chain mail**. They had steel weapons, and their ships had cannons. Many of them used **crossbows** and **harquebuses** (HAHR-kwih-buhs-ehs) in battle.

The conquistadors were **ruthless**. Beginning in 1519, they spent two years tearing through the New World. They ruined great empires like the Aztecs, Inkas, and Mayas. Along the way, they claimed land for Spain.

Conquistadors claimed most of Central and South America. But they were not finished. They had heard tales of gold in the north. In 1533, conquistador Hernán Cortés (her-NAHN cor-TEHS) sent some of his men to explore the coast. These were the first Europeans to set foot in Baja California, but they thought it was an island. The men named the land *California* after a queen from a famous Spanish book.

crossbow

Conquistadors wore iron suits of armor.

Hidalgos

Some conquistadors were also noblemen. Those soldiers were called *hidalgos* (hee-DALL-gohz). They kept horses and weapons ready so they could fight when they were called to serve.

Cortés the Conqueror

Cortés was one of the first conquistadors. He and his men explored Mexico. He wrote about his adventures in letters he sent back to Spain. These letters made him a legend in Spain.

Cortés and his men battle in Mexico.

The Colorado River

Francisco De Ulloa traveled up the West Coast until he reached shallow waters. **Sandbars** blocked his path, and he could go no farther. While there, he noticed a strong **current** in the water around him. He thought that a river must be flowing nearby. He was right. He had discovered the Colorado River **delta**.

Geography

This picture of the Colorado River delta was taken from space.

The Strait of Anián

The conquistadors were not the only Spanish explorers to come to the New World. Other sailors searched for a sea route that connected the Atlantic and Pacific Oceans. The English called this route the *Northwest Passage*. The Spanish knew it as the *Strait of Anián*. But there was no sea route. No one knew that because they did not have accurate maps. The only way to know the truth was to sail to the New World in person.

Spanish explorer Francisco de Ulloa (deh oo-YOH-ah) set out to find the Strait of Anián in 1539. First, he sailed up the coast of Mexico. Then, he went back down and around the coast of what is now Baja California. After that, he sailed south around the tip of South America and went back to Spain. He did not find the sea route. But he did prove that Baja California was not an island.

The Northwest Passage

Henry Hudson was an English explorer. He was one of many people who set out to find the Northwest Passage. All of Hudson's trips failed, and no sea route was ever found. Today, both the Hudson River and the Hudson Bay in New York are named after him.

In 1610, Hudson lands in what is now Canada.

Cabrillo's California

No one knows where or when Juan Rodríguez Cabrillo (HWAHN roh-DREE-gehz cah-BREE-yoh) was born. Most people think it was around 1475. Some say he was an orphan. His childhood is a mystery. One thing that is not a mystery is his impact on California's future.

Cabrillo's first known voyage was to the West Indies. He sailed with Pánfilo de Narváez (PAHN-fee-loh deh nahr-VAH-ehz) to Cuba. After that first trip, Cabrillo was hooked. Though he was young, he was a skilled warrior. Those skills helped convince Narváez to take Cabrillo on other trips. The two sailed together several times.

When Narváez set sail in 1520, Cabrillo went with him. The crew was going to Mexico. Their goal was to arrest Cortés for not following the king's orders. After Narváez was defeated, Cabrillo switched sides! He joined Cortés's conquistadors. Cabrillo marched through Mexico. Then, he went to live in what is now Guatemala.

Hernán Cortés

Arresting Cortés

The Spanish governor of Cuba was not happy when he heard Cortés's trade voyage had turned violent. He sent Narváez to arrest him for **treason**. Cortés heard about the plan. He surprised Narváez's crew at night. Narváez had four times as many soldiers as Cortés. But Cortés's surprise attack gave him the victory.

Civics

Map of the West Indies

Grand Galleon

In 2011, the San Diego Maritime Museum began to build a **replica** of the *San Salvador*. It took four years to complete. The ship is 92 feet (28 meters) long and 24 feet (7 meters) wide. As with the original, the model is made from wood. When the masts are up, it's 60 feet (18 meters) high.

The replica of the *San Salvador* is open for tours.

Setting Sail

On June 27, 1542, Cabrillo set sail on a new quest. He was hoping to find treasures and the Strait of Anián. He and his crew set sail on three ships, with Cabrillo on the *San Salvador*. Cabrillo used the most accurate maps of the time. This helped him navigate the rugged coast.

He sailed up the coast of Mexico. Sometimes, they had to wait a few days for the winds to change. Having the winds blow in the right direction would push them along faster. The journey was long. But they were excited about what they might find! Three months after the journey began, they entered what is now San Diego Bay. Cabrillo had arrived in California! He named the bay *San Miguel*.

Naming San Diego

Cabrillo and his crew landed in San Diego Bay on September 28, 1542. That is the Catholic feast day for the angel Saint Michael. Cabrillo named the bay *San Miguel* in honor of that day. It would be called San Miguel Bay for 60 years.

Geography

California Is Found!

Cabrillo and his crew stayed in San Miguel Bay for six days. Then, they sailed north past Santa Catalina Island. Next, they landed in San Pedro Bay, just south of what is now Los Angeles. They were the first Europeans to set foot on any of these lands.

They next discovered Santa Barbara and the Channel Islands. The Chumash tribe that lived there told Cabrillo about a large river up north. Cabrillo thought this might be the shortcut to Asia they were looking for. He took his crew and sailed north again.

The crew faced bad weather and rough storms the farther north they went. At one point, the *San Salvador* was separated from Cabrillo's other two ships. But the men kept sailing north. Some scholars think Cabrillo reached as far north as the Russian River, near Santa Rosa. But the storms were too harsh, and the crew turned back. On their return trip to the Channel Islands, Cabrillo was injured. He died soon after from health problems. His discovery of California would make him a legend.

Nobody Knows

Cabrillo died on San Miguel Island, one of the Channel Islands. Reports say he is buried on the island. But nobody knows for sure. Nobody even knows exactly how he died. Some reports say it was from a broken arm. Other reports say it was from a broken leg. The injury got infected and made him very sick. Cabrillo never recovered.

The Cabrillo monument overlooks San Diego Bay.

New Explorations

The leaders of Spain did not think much of Cabrillo's discovery. After all, he had not found the Strait of Anián. And the rumors about cities of gold seemed to be false. Spain's leaders had no interest in California, and they left it alone for years. Then, England sent Sir Francis Drake to the New World. He claimed California for England in 1579. After that, Spain's leaders wanted the land again.

Discovering Drake's Bay

Sir Francis Drake was an English explorer. He was also a pirate! He raided Spanish ships and stole their treasures. Drake anchored his ship in Point Reyes, north of San Francisco. Today, that place is called Drake's Bay.

In 1602, Sebastián Vizcaíno (se-vahs-TYAHN viz-kah-EE-noh) left New Spain for California. The Spanish wanted him to make an exact map of the area. He was also supposed to find a new port for trade. It took him six months to get to San Miguel Bay. When he landed, Vizcaíno renamed the bay *San Diego*. He went farther north and found Monterey Bay. Vizcaíno reported the bay as “the best port that one could hope for.” But he was wrong. His review of the bay was so misleading that future ships passed right by it. The crews of those ships could not believe that they were looking at the bay Vizcaíno had described.

Breaking the Rules

Vizcaíno was told not to change any of the names Cabrillo had given to the **landmarks** he found. But he did anyway! He claimed that Cabrillo's descriptions of the land were not accurate. Vizcaíno's names are the ones people still use today. These include San Diego Bay and the Carmel River.

Monterey Bay is one of the places where Vizcaíno landed.

Settling California

After Vizcaíno's trip to California, Spanish leaders left the region alone once again. Europeans did not return for over a century. In 1741, Vitus Bering found Alaska for Russia. He and his crew searched the state for furs to trade. Though Bering died that year, his crew kept searching. The next year, they left Alaska. They went south to look for more fur.

British and Spanish leaders heard news of the Russians moving south. This news troubled them. Leaders in both countries thought California belonged to them. They feared that Russian explorers would place a third claim on the land.

Early trips had not secured the land for Spain. The explorers did not form any settlements in the state. Spain's king knew he had to act fast. He sent a ship in 1769. The crew's goal was to settle the land for Spain. Soldiers and Catholic priests were among the crew. The priests had heard tales of native people living in California. They thought it was their job to **convert** these people to the Catholic faith.

Bering Strait

Bearing the Bering Name

Bering was an explorer from Denmark. He sailed the northern Pacific Coast on behalf of Russia. He made many great discoveries. Today, the Bering Strait and the Bering Sea are both named after him.

Geography

Why the Change?

England is part of a group of countries. In 1707, Scotland, England, and Wales joined together to become *Great Britain*. In 1801, Northern Ireland joined, too. The group became known as the United Kingdom. Today, both *Great Britain* and *United Kingdom* are still used to refer to the groups.

Explorers used tools to sail on the oceans.

California Indians

The Spanish began settling the region in 1769. At that time, there were over 300,000 California Indians in the area. American Indians had lived on the land for thousands of years. These tribes had their own languages and **cultures**.

California tribes had chosen their homes for specific reasons. They used landmarks such as streams, mountains, lakes, and trails to mark where they lived. The tribes used materials around them to build their homes. Everything from clothes to weapons came from the land.

The land also defined how they lived. If tribes were near lakes or streams, they fished. If their land had a lot of trees, they ate acorns. Most tribes hunted and gathered their food. They were careful not to hunt or fish too much. They wanted to make sure there was enough food for all people.

When Catholic priests started to build **missions**, they chose places near where tribes lived. This way, it would be easy to stay in contact with the tribes. These missions became the first major settlements in California.

Special Skills

The Chumash tribe lived near Santa Barbara. They lived close to the ocean, so they knew the sea very well. Their huts (shown here) were domed and made of grass. The Chumash made plank canoes and paddles. They also made stone tools and baskets.

Lost Traditions

Spanish settlers met a number of tribes in the San Francisco Bay area. When the Spanish took over, they forced these tribes and others to give up their ways of life. Many of the tribes' dances, languages, and other customs were lost. Below, is a drawing of a traditional dance from the Muwekma Ohlone Indians. This tribe has survived by teaching their language and customs to younger generations.

Mission San Juan Capistrano

San Juan Bautista

In 1797, the mission at San Juan Bautista was founded. It was built along the San Andreas **fault**. The church is the largest of all the missions built by the Spanish. This mission was well known for its American Indian boys' choir.

The Spanish built 21 missions in California. But Spain would soon lose control of the land. In 1821, Mexico broke from Spain. Mexican leaders split up the mission lands. They gave **land grants** to farmers. They hoped this would help secure the land. More settlers came to the state.

Then, the United States wanted California. It fought a war with Mexico. In 1848, both countries agreed to a deal, and the war ended. Mexico sold its land to the United States. More people came to California.

That same year, gold was found at Sutter's Mill. People from around the world **flooded** into this area. The true value of California was not realized right away. Instead, it took 300 years after Cabrillo sailed into San Miguel Bay for people to see what it was worth.

Mission San Antonio

300 Years of History

California is one of the most **diverse** states. Its history played a large role in this. Since no single country ruled the land, many people from different backgrounds settled there.

California Today

California has much to offer. It has a warm climate, fertile lands, scenic beaches, and more. It is hard to believe that Spanish explorers did not see the region's value when they first found it. They thought they would find cities paved with gold. When they did not, they left. When they came back 100 years later, the world finally saw California's riches.

Many countries fought for the land over the next 200 years. Their leaders even went to war for it. At times, the region belonged to Spain, England, Russia, and Mexico. In 1848, the United States won the land.

Today, California is the richest state in the nation. It also has more people than any other state. The countries that once claimed the area can be seen in the state's diverse people.

Where's the Bay?

The San Francisco Bay is larger than San Diego and San Jose combined. But explorers had a hard time finding it. Many explorers sailed right past it. The fog made it hard to find. Gaspar de Portolá (deh por-toh-LAH), a Spanish military officer, finally discovered it in 1769. But he reached the bay by land, not by water.

Geography

Sketch It!

When explorers were traveling to new lands, they relied on the stars, the sun, and maps to find their way. But those maps were not always accurate. Now, it is your turn to make a map for others to use.

First, walk around your neighborhood. Make note of any landmarks that would be easy for others to identify. Landmarks could be trees, playgrounds, parking lots, or houses. These things do not move. Don't put people or cars on your map because they do not stay in the same places all the time.

Pick one of your landmarks as a tool to measure distance for your map. Once you have made your notes, sketch your neighborhood. Add color and a key. When you are creating the map, do not use any tools that explorers during the Age of Discovery did not have. That means you cannot use the Internet or modern map books.

Then, trade maps with a friend. See if you can find a point in his or her neighborhood by only using the map.

GRAN QUIVIRA
MOQUI
LAS CALIFORNIAS O CAROLINAS
MAR DEL

LA FLORIDA
LVCAYA

California
Fort Crook
Fort Reading
Downieville
Nevada City
Sutter's Fort
Gold Rush Country 1849
San Francisco Solano 1823
San Francisco de Asis 1776
Cabrillo 1542
Drake 1579
Viscaino 1602
Portola-Serra 1769
Anza 1774

Part of North America

Glossary

chain mail—a type of protective clothing made from metal rings that have been linked together

conquistadors—Spanish soldiers during the sixteenth century

convert—to change from one religion or belief to another

crossbows—weapons that shoot arrows

cultures—the beliefs and ways of groups of people

current—a nonstop movement of air or water in the same direction

delta—a piece of land that is formed when a river splits into smaller rivers before it flows into an ocean

diverse—made up of things that are different from each other

empires—groups of countries that are controlled by one ruler

fault—a crack in Earth's surface

flooded—arrived in huge numbers

harquebuses—early guns that were heavy and rested on tripods

land grants—contracts that give ownership of plots of land

landmarks—objects or structures that are easy to see and can serve as guides to mark locations

landmass—a large piece of land, such as a continent

masts—long poles that hold the sails of boats or ships

missions—places or buildings where religious work is done

myth—a story that is believed by many people but is not true

replica—an exact or close copy of something

rival—a person or team that competes with another

ruthless—showing no pity or mercy

sandbars—raised areas of sand with tops that are near or right above the surface of bodies of water

treason—the crime of betraying one's own country

Index

Your Turn!

Symbolic Shield

A coat of arms is a group of symbols and colors shown on a shield. It represents a person or family. In the upper-left hand corner of the picture is Cortés's coat of arms.

Create your own coat of arms. Draw a shield and divide it into four sections. Think of four symbols and colors that represent you or your family. Place at least one symbol and color in each section. Include a written explanation of the symbols and colors you chose.